Scotland's First GOLFER?
~Hugh Kennedy of Ardstinchar ~

Jean Brittain

Carraig Books 2016

Copyright © 2016 Jean Brittain

All rights reserved. No part of this publication may be reproduced,
distributed, or transmitted in any form or by any means,
or stored in a database or retrieval system,
without the prior written permission of the author.

To my children
Lois and Camran
who once wore Scottish school uniforms in the
historic azure and gold colours of France
and came on many journeys to find out why

Ailsa Craig

Ardstinchar Castle

BALLANTRAE

Ballantrae sits on Scotland's Ayrshire coast, south of Turnberry and Troon and likewise dominated by the iconic landmark island of Ailsa Craig. The village and its environs were the ancient domain of the mighty Kennedys of Bargany & Ardstinchar. All that remains is their mausoleum – and the ruins of Ardstinchar Castle at the end of the busy Main Street.

This fortress on its rocky crag was once the principal seat of these barons. It was built in the 15th century and lasted intact until around 1770 when most of its stones were quarried for recycling into the building of the old bridge. What's left of the tower and courtyard now slowly crumbles away with the years like an old man shedding baggage on his final journey home.

What few folks realise is that Hugh Kennedy, its original financier, has a curious link to the beginning of golf in Scotland.

Grand debates rage about how ancient pastimes such as French chole, Dutch kolf or even Chinese chuiwan developed into modern golf, and the accidental loss of a ball down a rabbit-hole seems as good a theory for that light-bulb moment as any. The Scots claim to have made getting the ball into a hole the object of the game, and to have invented the links course.

"There can be no doubt that it was in Scotland that the game of golf, as we now know it, evolved and it is to Scotland that golf owes its cultural continuity."

Origins of Golf, British Golf Museum at St Andrews

When I researched Hugh Kennedy of Ardstinchar for a biography, I was stunned to find his name turning up at the very start of the timeline of Scottish golf. This man's life is astounding enough and the golf part is just an extra chapter, but it's a quirky story worth the telling.

Let me take you back to the early 15th century, to the days of smooth chivalry and rough pillaging and the chance for the nobility to make much coin as hired swords in foreign countries. Hugh Kennedy's story will give you a feel for living in those times, and I'll explain the connection between the royal and ancient game in Scotland and the Battle of Baugé in France.

Firstly we need to establish three dates in history, because the whole point is about *when* golf got started in Scotland.

15th century
Timeline of Scottish Golf

FOOTBALL BANNED — 1421 1424

Battle of Baugé "playing at ball"

1430   1440   1450

GOLF BANNED — 1457

Scotland's First GOLFER?
- Hugh Kennedy of Ardstinchar -

James I, King of Scots, banned football in 1424 because it hindered the practising of archery for military training. In 1457, his son King James II added golf to the football ban for the same reason. Something happened in the intervening thirty-three years to make this new game of 'gowf' so popular with the Scots that the distraction of it was threatening national security.

The credit is widely given to mercenary soldiers, in particular **Hugh Kennedy, Robert Stewart of Railston and John Smale of Aberdeen,** for bringing a game home from France to Scotland where it developed into golf. That theory is based on what Hugh and his comrades were doing just before the Battle of Baugé in 1421.

The battle was a huge victory for the Scots mercenaries who'd gone there under the Auld Alliance to help the French fight the English. The Scots even killed the Duke of Clarence who was the Regent of France and heir to the throne of England held by his brother King Henry V.

Here's what the Book of Pluscarden said about it around 1460. The author was a monk who had either been at the battle or had a detailed eyewitness account of it. It certainly sounds like a good game of golf interrupted...

"Yet on the eve of the said Easter Festival, while the Scots thought no evil, nay, were utterly free from falseness and deceit, and were **playing at ball** and amusing themselves with other pleasant or devout occupations, all of a sudden the English chiefs treacherously rushed upon them from an ambush while they were almost unarmed. But by God's mercy some **men of note were playing at a passage over a certain river,** and they caught sight of their banners coming stealthily in ambush ...

So these English... **were attacked first at the passage by Hugh Kennedy, Robert Stewart of Railston and John Smale of Aberdeen**, with their followers"

F Skene (Editor), *The Book of Pluscarden* – Edinburgh 1880

Golf historian Robert Browning reasoned that this "playing at ball" must have been some cross-country game because the group were so far from the main camp, because there were so few players, and because **'men of note'** like Hugh Kennedy wouldn't be so likely to join in football or shinty. His best guess was that the Scots had taken up the local game of ***chole***:

"If they learned it in this campaign, brought it back to Scotland, and transformed it into golf, the dates would fit. The chole of 1421 might easily have developed into golf in time to become widely popular by 1457."

R Browning, *A History of Golf: The Royal and Ancient Game* – London 1955

Olive Geddes noted that the golf may have been an accidental omission in the Scottish ban. King James I had recently returned from captivity in England, and his 1424 ban on football largely reiterated an English decree from 1363. But she also wrote:

"It could, however, indicate that a significant rise in the popularity of golf in Scotland had occurred sometime during the second quarter of the fifteenth century."

O M Geddes, *A Swing Through Time: Golf in Scotland 1457-1744* – Edinburgh 2007

I'm going to tell you about Hugh Kennedy to show how his career path, coupled with the belief systems of the 15th century, can put a whole different slant on the men's **'playing at ball'**, and then we'll take a fresh look at that and more.

Religion came into everything then – and into Hugh's life far more than most.

Scotland's First GOLFER?
- Hugh Kennedy of Ardstinchar -

'He wes callit Freir Hew...'
Historie of the Kennedyis, manuscript written early 1600s
ADV MS 33.3.28 at the National Library of Scotland

Hugh Kennedy was born in the 1390s at Dunure Castle, just south of Ayr. He was one of the nine sons of Sir Gilbert Kennedy of Dunure in a powerful family which ruled Carrick. As the *third* son of his father's second marriage to Dame Agnes Maxwell, he might have grown up expecting to be destined for a life in the church. Not the case for Hugh.

We know about his early career because of a letter he sent to the Pope in later life. It's an absolute diatribe against the Dominican Order of the Friars Preachers, known as the Blackfriars.

He says he was sent to school at the Blackfriars Monastery in Ayr (just a few miles from Dunure) at the age of sixteen to learn Latin, but the Blackfriars deceived him into entering their monastery and wearing the habit. Tellingly, the Blackfriars kept him away from his parents for several years, even transferring him to England until he reached the required ages to be pushed into taking the irrevocable vows as a subdeacon and then deacon without parental permission.

The Blackfriars then brought him back to Scotland and again *'incited him'*, this time to receive the order of priest, before he could consult with his parents who were *'of the stock of King James and his kinsmen, and powerful and great'*. Hugh was indeed related in the fourth degree of kindred on both sides to King James I.

It was a crime to leave a monastery without authorisation. Religious runaways were branded vagabonds and apostates. If arrested, they could be imprisoned and held in iron chains. Hugh was 27 years old by the time he received parental permission to *'return to the world'*, and went to France as a mercenary.

Of course, there were political agendas going on at this time which affected Scotland and France very much, and the Kennedys of Dunure in particular. As we'll see later, this background story would also influence Hugh's actions just prior to the Battle of Baugé.

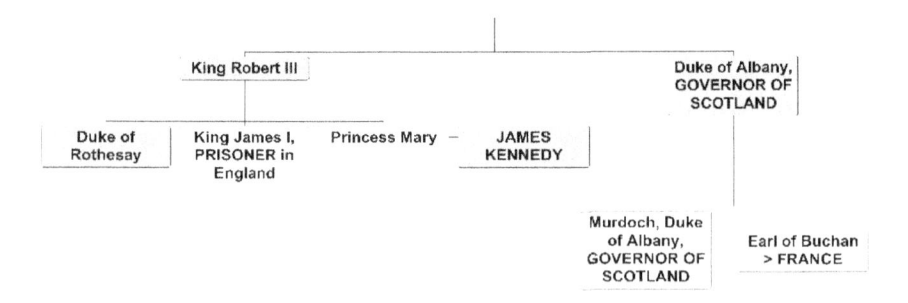

```
                          |
      ┌───────────────────┴──────────────┐
   King Robert III                  Duke of Albany,
                                    GOVERNOR OF
                                    SCOTLAND
 ┌────────┬──────────────┐
Duke of  King James I,  Princess Mary  —  JAMES
Rothesay PRISONER in                     KENNEDY
         England
                                    Murdoch, Duke
                                    of Albany,         Earl of Buchan
                                    GOVERNOR OF        > FRANCE
                                    SCOTLAND
```

Hugh's brother James Kennedy had wed the king's daughter Princess Mary, but was killed in mortal combat with an elder half-brother over the chieftainship of Clan Kennedy. The half-brother fled to France and died there.

The Duke of Rothesay, heir to the Scottish throne, was also dead – starved to death by his uncle the Duke of Albany.

King Robert III died within weeks of hearing that his other son James had been captured at sea on his way to safety in France. The Duke of Albany became Governor of Scotland and was in no hurry to ransom the young King James out of English captivity.

Around the time that our Hugh was sent to the Blackfriars Monastery school in Ayr, his father Sir Gilbert Kennedy of Dunure had signed allegiance to this Duke of Albany – and Dunure Castle was at stake. The man running the Blackfriars Monastery in Ayr was Finlay of Albany, the Duke of Albany's confessor.

So it's fair to say that Hugh was a hostage for his father's allegiance, especially because the old Duke of Albany and his confessor Finlay both came out of the picture the same year that Hugh came out of the monastery... and because the man who took Hugh to France as a hired sword was the Earl of Buchan, brother of the new Duke of Albany & Governor of Scotland.

Some of Hugh's disinherited half-brothers might also have been keen enough for the Blackfriars to keep him all those years. Being hustled into Holy Orders took yet another contender out of the running to be chief of Clan Kennedy, even temporarily until a nephew came of age.

The author of the family history, without access to the Vatican Archives, wrote:

"The house of Bargany came to their preferment by the valour of a second brother who was first put to have been a Friar; but his courage, not agreeable to so base an office, left the same, and passed with the Lord of Buchan to France, to Charles the VII, in the year of our Lord 1421. He was called Friar Hew, and was, for his valour, so beloved of the King of France that he remained with him many years thereafter..."

Historie of the Kennedyis, written early 1600s
[Translated from Late Middle Scots language and edited for transcription errors]

Many later authors have treated Hugh as a lad who ran off from a monastery for a bit of swashbuckling and ended up a notable captain, such authors unaware that he arrived in France as a fully-ordained priest of the Dominican Order of Friars Preachers. Hugh can't have been ignorant of the underlying politics by the time he wrote to the Pope, but doubtless it suited his own agenda by then to blame the Blackfriars.

Hugh was excommunicated, but there's nothing in the papal records to say he'd been relieved of the burdens of priesthood. He'd barely arrived in France with the Earl of Buchan and thousands of other Scots mercenaries when the Battle of Baugé happened. There he was, playing at ball with his pals, when the English army broke the Easter truce and ambushed them.

In that supposed three-ball in 1421 we have, in name order:

- **Hugh Kennedy** – an excommunicated priest, remembered in his family history as 'Friar Hew'.

- **Robert Stewart of Railston** – Hugh's second cousin. They shared Walter, 6th Steward of Scotland, as a common ancestor. Ralston, near Glasgow, was only about five miles from the Pollok home of Hugh's mother Agnes Maxwell. The Stewarts of Darnley lived in this area too, so we see the family and local connections among the leaders of the men landing in France. Little if anything more is known about Robert Stewart.

- **John Smale of Aberdeen**, about whom nothing at all is known.

Years later, Hugh was on the front line at the Siege of Montargis while his new commanding officer (John Stewart of Darnley, mentioned above) was thirty miles away. The Siege of Orléans began in 1428, and it would go on for seven months. The English were spaced out around the city, and Hugh forced his way in for a convoy of food to get through. And then disaster struck.

They called it the Battle of the Herrings, albeit a hundred miles from the sea. The English besiegers themselves needed provisions for Lent when meat was forbidden, so an army was sent from Paris with a long line of wagons laden with salted herrings and other permitted foods.

The Franco-Scots army outnumbered the English. The wagon line was there for the taking. Hugh Kennedy and Sir William Stewart wanted to attack the convoy at once, but out of deference they sent for orders to their French commander, an inexperienced young noble who ordered them to wait. Sir John Stewart of Darnley, Constable of the Scots, eventually disobeyed the order but the delay had given the English time to prepare. The Scots and French were slaughtered.

It was a major defeat, so bad that the French king talked about running away to Scotland. The Franco-Scots army fell into disarray. Hugh survived and is recorded out pillaging with *'fully 800 horse'* so it seems he'd been left with rather a lot of empty-bellied Scots after the Battle of the Herrings.

This is when Joan of Arc came on the scene. She was a teenager on a divine mission and the Hundred Years War became even more about whose side God was on.

Hugh Kennedy was Joan of Arc's Scottish Captain with the Garde Ecossaise. There were other Scottish captains in Orléans, but he was the only one at the Council of War where plans were hatched to tackle the English besiegers.

A local 'Mystery Play' performed in the years after the siege lists only four Scots. John Stewart of Darnley (Constable of the Scots) and his brother William were killed at the Battle of the Herrings so they never met Joan of Arc. John Kirkmichael was the Bishop of Orléans. Hugh Kennedy is listed as the 'Captain of the Scots in the service of the king'.

He was prominent at the Storming of the Tourelles – that was the main battle scene of the siege, although the Scots never seem to get a mention in the Joan of Arc movies.

The Siege of Orléans was lifted, and on they went, taking town after town back from the English. Hugh was in the royal escort when King Charles braved the journey through English-held territory to Rheims for proper coronation, necessary because of the Holy Oil of Clovis there.

Paris was still held by the English. Hugh was made head of the Scots garrison at Lagny-sur-Marne which guarded one of the main approaches, and he'd be there for several years.

It was Lagny that Joan of Arc went to when the French king let her down. She said *"the men there wage good war against the English"*. She was right, and Hugh's name is among the captains raiding up to the walls of Paris and laying ambushes. It was when Joan moved on from Lagny that she was captured, tried, and burned at the stake. She wasn't hanged. The English had her killed as a heretic to prove God was on their side.

Hugh had been alongside Joan in a fight with the English near Lagny, and that's why he gets a mention in the record of her trial.

One of Joan's 'voices' was Saint Catherine of Alexandria, the very saint that the Blackfriars Monastery in Ayr was dedicated to. You can see this saint on the monastery's 1406 seal with her wheel and sword.

Lagny itself came under attack in 1432 in a long and bitter siege. The people were starving. One French soldier later spoke about eating his own horse there. Hugh's name is at the top of the list of captains who fought off the first wave of English and their heavy siege guns under the command of the Earl of Arundel. Here's what a chronicler said at the time:

> "They advanced gallantly to storm the place; but by the vigilance and intrepidity of Huçon Queue [*Hugh Kennedy*], a Scotsman, Sir John Foucault, and the other captains in the town, they were boldly received, and very many of the assailants were killed or severely wounded."
>
> *The Chronicles of Enguerrand de Monstrelet: Vol 1* – London 1853

The Duke of Bedford was furious and arrived to take charge in person. Hugh was now up against the English Regent of France. This was the man who'd sent Joan of Arc to the stake, and the Scots had already killed his brother the Duke of Clarence at the Battle of Baugé thirteen years previously.

Reinforcements arrived for the French side. The English were eventually tricked by a decoy and headed off to Paris, and were made to look a bit foolish when the guys from the Lagny garrison nipped out and stole all their supplies.

Hugh Kennedy gets special mention in the Annals of Lagny for being a captain of great skill and cleverness at this siege – *"un capitaine écossais, d'une grande habileté, nommé Huçon Kennedy"*. The French king then put him onto diplomatic work, though it was far from being a medieval desk job.

King James I
father of the bride

King Charles VII
father of the groom

In the winter of 1434 a French embassy set sail for the court of King James in Scotland. Their mission: to fetch the Scots Princess Margaret, aged ten, to marry the French Dauphin Louis, aged 12.

Hugh Kennedy was now Squire of the Royal Stables for King Charles VII of France who chose him as an ambassador, obviously for his Scottish nationality and military prowess, but likely also for his language skills in English, French and Latin... and vernacular Scots. The manuscripts from this era show it as a language of its own which would definitely need a translator.

Sir Regnault Girard, the principal ambassador and Master of the Royal Household for the French king, was so terrified of this mission that he freely wrote in his diplomatic diary about offering a sizeable financial bribe to any man who would take his place. However, he conveniently owned a large ship and King Charles forced him to go. The third ambassador was the embassy's clerk chosen at the last minute by Girard – Aymery Martineau, a lawyer and Master of Requests for King Charles.

The embassy left La Rochelle and their ship got blown 200 miles into the Atlantic by a storm. So, when they finally made official landing at Loch Ryan, Hugh took them straight to the shrine of St Ninian at Whithorn in Galloway on pilgrimage where they left a votive offering of a silver ship.

Hugh then took the embassy to his home, maybe Dunure Castle, but far more likely Ardstinchar Castle run by his brother Thomas who was Baillie of Carrick at the time. Hugh gave them a grand feast and brought many of his family and friends – no doubt the same *'relations and friends, knights and squires'* he gathered up to give a prestigious escort to the embassy for their entry into Edinburgh, now made up of *'sixty horse and more'*.

When the embassy reached King James in Edinburgh, the negotiations didn't go well. King James stalled and wanted extra conditions. Somebody had to nip over to France and talk to King Charles.

Hugh Kennedy and the lawyer Martineau sailed off. The lawyer came back with letters. Hugh was gone six months, and came back with a fleet of ships.

But our King James stalled again while he negotiated with England. The Auld Alliance hung in the balance all winter.

This embassy had been going on for over a year by the time the Scots King finally committed to France in the spring of 1436. He consulted with the ambassadors on the princess's retinue for the voyage, the composition of the military escort and the safety measures for avoiding an intercept by the English.

The Admiral of the Fleet for this voyage was to be William Sinclair, 3rd Earl of Orkney – the same man who would soon being building Rosslyn Chapel. William Sinclair was only about 25 years old at the time of this embassy, and without experience in fighting outside of Scotland. Hugh Kennedy was in his early forties. He was a Scotsman in Scotland as a French Ambassador, and had a ferocious reputation abroad in cunning military strategy.

When the other two ambassadors went off to Dumbarton to the fleet, Hugh stayed behind in Perth for a fortnight to *"superintend the levying and equipping of the military force"*... while he was in the pay of the French.

Only two Scotsmen could have given Hugh such involvement when so many other Scottish knights and nobles were available – King James and Earl William Sinclair. Both men were related to him in the fourth degree of kindred on at least one parental line. As with Robert Stewart of Railston in the 'playing at ball', their common ancestor was Walter, 6th Steward of Scotland from whom the royal surname of Stewart originated.

About 1200 people gathered in Dumbarton ready to set sail with the princess – a bishop, knights, nobility and soldiers – and the best of Scottish finery was put on show by Earl William to be seen in France.

King James held a race to see which ship was the fastest, and that turned out to be the only Spanish ship in a fleet which was otherwise French. The French sailors threatened mutiny for the dishonour to their country, but King James still insisted on putting the princess on the Spanish ship.

Another ship arrived from France with provisions and gifts. The Scots queen was given barrels of wine and fruit. King James was presented with... a mule. On the surface this would be a religious gift. The young bridegroom Louis the Dauphin was born in the town of Bourges where the Feast of the Ass was particularly celebrated, and the coat of arms of Bourges was, would you believe, an ass seated in an armchair.

In those days, as now, there was the open meaning and the covert. The veiled barb was clear. King James's stubbornness was legend, and I suspect he might have preferred to receive that rather nice silver ship which went instead to Whithorn. The phrase *"He's like the Arms of Bourges"* did come into later French usage, and it meant *'an ignorant man in a big chair'* – an ass in a position of authority.

Hugh Kennedy captained an army ship called the Saint Giles for the voyage to France, away from the Scottish elite in their comfortable berths. We can imagine the majestic sight of this fleet sailing down the Clyde past Ailsa Craig, past all the Kennedy castles and King Robert the Bruce's old castle at Turnberry as they headed out for La Rochelle.

The diplomatic diary says nothing of an attempted intercept, but other sources do. The Duke of Gloucester sent 180 ships to capture the princess, no doubt spread around every conceivable route to La Rochelle.

The English nearly did manage near Brittany, but a fleet of wine ships from Flanders appeared and the English went after them instead. A fleet from Spain then turned up and rescued the Flemings. The English were left with nothing at all, and the princess reached France safely.

This surely cannot have been a coincidence, not when the King of Scots had put his daughter on the only Spanish ship that Hugh Kennedy had brought from France.

Another account says:

"The Scots bore the Princess Margaret safely into the port of La Rochelle pursued by English cruisers, but the entrance of the roads was closed in time by the help of some Castilian auxiliaries, of the embassy of Don Enrique."

C Hare, The Life of Louis XI – London 1907

The port of La Rochelle was once owned by the Knights Templar. This was the only major port the French had left so it's a mystery that the English never tried to take it back after 1372, not least to stop the supply of Scots mercenaries coming to the aid of King Charles.

King James's choice of the Spanish ship to carry the princess may well have been because of its top-speed capability to outrun pirates and its higher numbers of rowers in the event of being becalmed. That he chose it despite threat of mutiny by the French sailors, and that Admiral William Sinclair was made a Knight of the Cockle upon arrival, is highly suggestive of the covert involvement all along of a religious Military Order for the princess's safety.

"...when he was arrived in France, he was honoured of all men, and loved of the King, who made him Knight of the Cockle, after the ordre of France..."

Father R A Hay, Genealogie of the Sainteclaires of Rosslyn
(Edited by R L D Cooper) – Edinburgh 2002

Hugh had already fought alongside the Knights Hospitaller at the Siege of Orléans. Some say the Knights of St Lazarus were also at that siege.

Scotland's First GOLFER?
- Hugh Kennedy of Ardstinchar -

The Spanish Order of St James, also known as the Order of Santiago (academics still debate if it was one Order or two), had been founded in the 12th century to guard the various pilgrimage routes to the shrine of St James at Compostela. In the century previous to this embassy voyage they'd taken in many of the disbanded Knights Templar, same as the other Military Orders did.

Crucially for William Sinclair, the Knights of Santiago was the only religious Military Order of the era which allowed its members to be married. The Grand Master of the Order at the time of the embassy was the Infante Don Enrique of Castile and Leon – the 'Don Enrique' mentioned above whose Castilian auxiliaries came to the rescue.

The badge of the Knights of Santiago and the symbol of this pilgrimage was the clamshell/scallop known as the *'coquille'*, hence the Earl of Orkney was made Knight of the Cockle.

At some point during this embassy Hugh had petitioned the Pope, with a supporting petition from the king of France, asking to return to the church. It's in the papal decision that we hear of Hugh's reasons for leaving fifteen years earlier, told out in his diatribe against the Blackfriars. After the princess's wedding in the summer of 1436, Hugh became an *Augustinian* canon at the French monastery of St John the Evangelist at Sens to do his penance for being absent 15 years. He stayed in Holy Orders for the rest of his life.

⚜

Hugh Kennedy had come a long way from 'playing at ball' at a French riverside with his pals, but was it golf in any form that was being played by these three men just before the 1421 Battle of Baugé? I wish it was, but I don't think so.

I've highlighted much about religious beliefs and practices in the 15th century because I believe these men were playing a religious ball game. Let's take a fresh look at the facts in the Book of Pluscarden from that slant:

"Yet on the eve of the said **Easter Festival**, while the Scots thought no evil, nay, were utterly free from falseness and deceit, and were **playing at ball and amusing themselves with other pleasant or devout occupations**, all of a sudden the English chiefs treacherously rushed upon them from an ambush while they were almost unarmed. But by God's mercy some **men of note were playing at a passage over a certain river,** and they caught sight of their banners coming stealthily in ambush ... So these English... were attacked first at the passage by Hugh Kennedy, Robert Stewart of Railston and John Smale of Aberdeen, with their followers..."

- it was Easter Saturday

- they were *"playing at ball and amusing themselves with other pleasant or devout occupations"*

- they were playing at a passage over a river

The original Latin version of the Book of Pluscarden gives this 'playing at ball' as **'ad palmam ludentibus'**, the sense of which is more like playing with the palm of the hand. Tennis of that time was played without a racquet, and it was called *'jeu de paume'*.

Possibly the author was just avoiding mentioning golf because it was banned in Scotland by the time he came to write the chronicle, but again, I don't think so. The author took it for granted that the reader would know exactly what kind of handball game he meant without defining it. He was a monk in Pluscarden Priory when he wrote it, having returned from several years in French royal circles in the service of the very princess Hugh had taken there.

Another Scottish chronicle was written during the 1440s when Hugh was still alive by another churchman who knew Hugh's past and current life in Holy Orders. From this we can glean more facts:

- the Earl of Buchan's "...intention was to **attend divine service and office there until Easter Monday** out of reverence for the passion of Our Lord and the most central Christian communion service of the Eucharist..."

- the Scots "...**were in a sleepy state at about 3 o'clock in the afternoon**, but immediately roused themselves and flew to arms..."

- "...about a hundred Scots belonging to the retinue of Master Hugh Kennedy who were **lodged in a church nearby...**"

- the chronicler gives Hugh the title of **Master Hugh Kennedy** *(in Latin, **'magistri Hugonis Kenedy'**), which in that form usually indicated a graduate cleric

D E R Watt (Editor), *Scotichronicon by Walter Bower in Latin and English: Vol 8*
– Aberdeen 1987

It's my theory that the three men and their followers were 'playing at ball' in a labyrinth, and with one much bigger ball called a 'pilota'.

Labyrinths have enjoyed a great revival in recent years. This photo shows the spectacular stone one built recently by the villagers of Dunure at the castle where Hugh grew up – about ten miles up the coast from Turnberry.

Labyrinth patterns reach back at least four thousand years worldwide but they were Christianised by the church, as happened with the wells, standing stones, feast dates, etc. Scandinavian fishermen walked them to ensure favourable winds and fine catches by taking their troubles and worries to the centre and leaving them there. Today it is remembrances, hopes, wishes and votive offerings which are left behind in the centre of the maze.

In medieval cathedrals they called the labyrinth a 'pavement' and used it as a mini-pilgrimage known as 'The Path to Jerusalem'.

The labyrinth is all about allegory. In medieval times they based it on the twelve celestial spheres, but basically it's just the One True Path. There's only one inward route to the centre and the same outward journey in return as a changed person.

In pre-Christian times there was a labyrinth in the Greek legend of Theseus and the Minotaur. It's nothing to do with our Scottish gowf, but that Roman mosaic (above right) does look suspiciously like the Minotaur is about to get whacked by a golf bag and a club!

Some people called their labyrinth the 'House of Daedalus' – Daedalus being the architect of that Greek one with the Minotaur. By fifty years after the soldiers were *"playing at ball"* there's record of a labyrinth called Daedalus at the Castle of Baugé.

The turf maze was the same concept in the outdoors where space was easier to find and a plain labyrinth much cheaper to create. Even today, all that's needed is sacred geometry and a cleverly-driven lawnmower.

This grass one comes and goes at Whithorn Priory where Hugh took the French Embassy on pilgrimage all those centuries ago.

In medieval times there were many deeper-cut turf mazes, mainly near churches – and Hugh Kennedy's men were **"lodged in a church nearby"**.

At Easter only, at the end of Lent, labyrinths were used for playing a ball game in a throwback to the pagan rituals. This was the time for the clergy and congregation to have some fun after the restrictions of Lent, same as happened at the January Feast of Fools and the Feast of the Ass after Christmas.

The clergy joined hands to form a ring-dance, and chanted and danced into the labyrinth through all the twists and turns. The Dean danced in the centre and threw the pilota back and forth to them. There was even a Latin song-chant which went with it: *Victimae Paschali Laudes* – *"Praises for the Easter Victim"*.

Elements of the Dance of the Maze survive today in Breton Folk Dance where the mayor and the entire village population link arms and dance in the curving, weaving pattern of the labyrinth. In medieval times the dance was so integral to the ritual that I wonder if the dance-moves themselves were used as a way of trampling out a labyrinth pattern on a natural setting like grass or earth before the pilota was thrown. The moves in Breton Folk Dance certainly look to have been based on this purpose, with the linked line of people moving along in a curve, then stopping to 'trample' with rhythmic steps before moving on again, and with the linked line intermittently doubling back on itself.

Here's where the fun came in with the pilota ball...

- The leather pilota was of a definite minimum size so it was impossible to clutch it in one hand – it would have to be balanced on an upturned palm and be lobbed

- The leader could only use his LEFT ('sinister') hand, which was bound to further diminish the accuracy of his aim

- Some of the participants within the labyrinth's twists would be facing away from the leader when the ball was thrown, so they'd have to be warned to duck down

- The participants were dancing with their hands linked to their neighbours – so how could they return the ball to the leader? Tandem linked hands like volleyball? Headers? Footers? Good sport was to be had, for sure.

Hugh Kennedy had been with the Blackfriars for ten years just before he went to France. It was Easter Saturday, the end of the Lenten Fast. So... I would say he was leading his fellow captains and followers in the accepted Easter ball game, and on a riverside turf maze belonging to the nearby church he was using as a billet for his men.

His parents had given permission for him to leave the monastery, but they were still under allegiance to Murdoch, the new Duke of Albany & Governor of Scotland... whose brother the Earl of Buchan was Hugh's commanding officer, and intended the Easter weekend to be spent in devotions.

As an excommunicated friar and now a captain responsible for at least a hundred men-at-arms, Hugh might have made it his business to be seen leading an authorised religious game of an afternoon during the Easter devotions, rather than just lazing about 'in a sleepy state' as most of the other Scots were doing. He'd be the man who knew the pilota rules, and his name came first in the Book of Pluscarden for 'playing at ball'.

⚜

If my theory is correct, it's disappointing to wipe that 'playing at ball' clue from the history of Scottish golf. However... the Scots are sure to have played the local French game of *chole* at times outwith religious festivals, and the timeline still holds for golf's beginnings in Scotland somewhere over the years 1424-1457.

To be fair, any one or several of the homecoming survivors from the Hundred Years War could have brought the game back to Scotland. Hugh and his comrades only got the credit because the Book of Pluscarden just happened to mention what they were doing when the English attacked. That said, let's take a look at where Hugh was after his return to Holy Orders in 1436, over the years that Scottish golf was really taking off.

Whatever Hugh had done on that embassy earned him huge rewards from the kings of France and Scotland, much more than his two fellow ambassadors received.

After doing his penance in France, Hugh came back to Scotland. King James also petitioned the Pope on his behalf, but waited until after the princess was safely landed and married.

Together with a canonry of Aberdeen with the prebend of Turriff, here's what the king of Scots personally awarded to Hugh:

Kirkheugh

Kirkheugh – a rather fitting place-name. The Provostship, for life, of the Chapel Royal of St Mary on the Rock. Its foundations can be seen between the cathedral and harbour in St Andrews. Once a Culdee chapel, this was now the royal collegiate church with clergy devoted exclusively and constantly to the salvation of the royal family's souls.

Hugh had experience in the specialism of such family churches. His grandfather had built one in Maybole in the late 1300s, one of the first in Scotland. Known locally as 'The Auld College', the ruins still stand today with the Kennedy heraldry over the door.

Hugh's appointment to the Provostship of Kirkheugh brought with it a stall in the choir and a place in the chapter of St Andrews Cathedral, and a voice in the election of the bishop and other offices.

King James had entrusted Hugh with the safety of his firstborn child on her voyage to France. The king himself had been living in fear of his life, and was now entrusting Hugh with the immortal souls of himself and all his family. King James was right to be worried – he was assassinated in February 1437, less than a year after he'd sent his daughter to France.

By 1438, Hugh was also Treasurer of Glasgow, with which came the prebend of Carnwath and the fairly new collegiate church founded 1424 by Thomas Lord Somerville.

Hugh was Treasurer of Glasgow right over the time that William Sinclair, Earl of Orkney began planning and building Rosslyn Chapel, the collegiate church of the Sinclairs. Whatever was involved in Earl William's learning the necessary basics and garnering handy hints for building a collegiate church, it's well-documented that Rosslyn's layout was based on the East Quire of Glasgow Cathedral. Hugh would know much about collegiate churches, having grown up with his grandfather's in Maybole and now having two in his charge, and he had already worked closely with his kinsman Earl William in getting the young princess to France.

Scotland's First GOLFER?
- Hugh Kennedy of Ardstinchar -

Sir Gilbert Hay translated an old French poem into Scots around 1460 and called it *'The Buik of King Alexander the Conqueror'*. He was in the employ of Earl William, and the poem twice mentions golf. The game was certainly in the minds of these people. Gilbert Hay had also been in service at the French court with Hugh Kennedy, though he returned to Scotland later.

For those readers with interests in Rosslyn Chapel's associations to Freemasonry, I should add a note on the Kennedy Mausoleum (also known as the Bargany Aisle) in Hugh's village of Ballantrae.

When the local Masonic Lodge designed their penny, they honoured:

- ○ Ardstinchar Castle, looking east to west and adding a square to encompass the courtyard and village

- ○ the village's old bridge, made from the castle's quarried stones

- ○ Ailsa Craig

Masonic interest is perhaps connected to the Kennedy Mausoleum built in Ballantrae in 1604 for Gilbert Kennedy, the final great baron cut down in his prime. The same stonemason, David Scougal, is thought to have crafted both the Kennedy Mausoleum and the Dunfermline Abbey tomb for William Schaw who wrote the statutes for modern freemasonry.

As we'll see, two of the last Kennedy lairds of Bargany & Ardstinchar were known to be golfers, one of them before 1597.

※

Hugh's service to the royalty of Scotland and France continued to be rewarded by permissions to earn as much as he wanted and to do whatever he felt like. Kingship, politics and the church were inseparable in those days, much to his financial benefit. He gathered up benefices in Forteviot, and Wigtown, and the promise of a canonry of Moray or Dunkeld. The Pope allowed him to, because the kings of France and Scotland kept backing him up. He had special permission from the Pope to earn up to £500 a year – an absolute fortune back then.

The Kennedy feud had already begun between two or perhaps three factions within the families of the nine sons of the late Sir Gilbert Kennedy of Dunure.

In 1429, during Hugh's summer with Joan of Arc, Hugh had used proctors at home to combine his inherited lands of Ardstinchar with the Kirkoswald lands of his brother Thomas into the Barony of Ardstinchar. The royal charter was witnessed by William Sinclair, 3rd Earl of Orkney, so he knew of Hugh's background even before they worked together on delivering the princess to France.

This side of the Kennedy family would later be known as the Bargany & Ardstinchar faction when Thomas fell heir to more lands. Money was required, and Hugh's high earning capability would be the ideal answer.

He went between Scotland and France and was Counsellor to both kings. King Charles of France even gave him the Lordship of Gournay-sur-Marne just a few miles from his old garrison at Lagny. A French king also awarded him the honour of quartering his Kennedy coat-of-arms with the single fleur-de-lys, though my research on the original manuscript of the family history tends towards this king being René d'Anjou – again, the connection to Earl William Sinclair would show here.

Hugh was still Treasurer of Glasgow when the University was founded by Bishop Turnbull in 1451, and then he moved up again. He became Archdeacon of St Andrews, where his nephew was now the famous Bishop James Kennedy... from the other main faction in the Kennedy feud.

The feud itself is a whole other story, but Hugh's branch of the family being the losing side affected his own reputation badly in later years. Within Balfour Paul's 'Scots Peerage' is an utter myth: *'He was nicknamed 'Come with the penny' (Venez avec le sou), a sobriquet given him on his return to his native land laden with money and honours given him by the French king.'*

As appropriate as that moniker sounds for a rich priest sounds, it isn't true. The nickname comes from a mistake made by the 17th century copyist of the family history, and the bigger truth was also ignored by authors who should have known better. The section actually reads, in Late Middle Scots language, *'This Freir Hewis oy wes callit Com with the Penny'*. The copyist merely misread one letter. It's not 'Com' – it's **Tom**. Further, the wee word **'oy'** in Scots means a grandson or nephew, which all peerage authors definitely knew.

Friar Hew did indeed have a grand-nephew known as **'Tom the Penny'**...

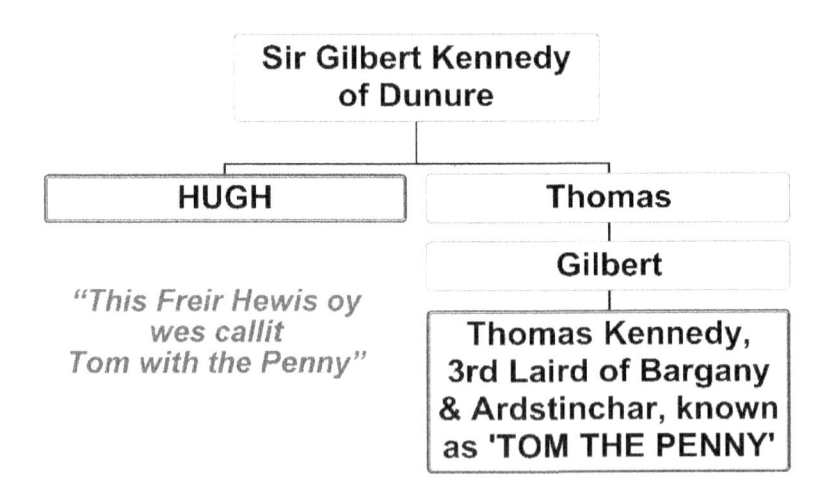

```
                    Sir Gilbert Kennedy
                        of Dunure
                            |
              ┌─────────────┴─────────────┐
            HUGH                       Thomas
                                          |
                                       Gilbert
                                          |
   "This Freir Hewis oy         Thomas Kennedy,
       wes callit               3rd Laird of Bargany
    Tom with the Penny"         & Ardstinchar, known
                                as 'TOM THE PENNY'
```

The proof of that lies in a 1562 legal document held by the National Records of Scotland in Edinburgh, where this man is referred to twice as the late *'Thomas Kenedy of Bargany callit Thom the Penny'*. The document is written in plain Scots, not Latin, and it's in the GD25 series known as the Ailsa Muniments – the papers of the Kennedy Family, Earls of Cassillis. That Kennedy branch won the clan feud, and its successive leaders hold the title Marquess of Ailsa and Chief of the Name of Kennedy. The Bargany & Ardstinchar faction lost, and their muniments are sparse affairs.

A pen and a print-run being mightier than the sword, Hugh's reputation was severely tarnished after publication of the Scots Peerage in 1905.

As far as I can find, his association with the history of golf did not come under discussion until much later. It is the winning side of the clan feud who must be given credit for creating the links golf course on their Turnberry lands in 1901, with the Ailsa Course named after the 3rd Marquess of Ailsa whose ancestor had taken the name from the isle of Ailsa Craig which they also owned.

But there's still more to tell about Hugh Kennedy's part in Scotland's golf history. His castle of Ardstinchar had a links course about three centuries before the Turnberry course came into official being.

⚜

"The immediate approach to Ballantrae is flat grassland, ideal ground for a Kennedy chief to muster his spearmen, but today occupied as a golf course"

D C Cuthbertson, *'Carrick Days'* – Edinburgh 1933

Scotland takes the credit for inventing links golf, so let's revisit Ballantrae down the Ayrshire coast from the renowned courses at Turnberry and Troon.

Three different golf courses including a links course have been known to exist at Ballantrae at various times, rather a consistent presence for such a small place far from any town, and especially in the days when transport was by horse or wobbly charabanc.

Hugh inherited Ardstinchar in the 1420s and built the castle after his return to Scotland. Ardstinchar Castle was the main stronghold for the Kennedys of Bargany & Ardstinchar and their extensive lands.

Round the corner from the castle on the north side of the village, there is a two-mile stretch of beachfront grass with the A77 running through it and a fine view of Ailsa Craig. The headland at its end was once owned by the Kennedys of Bennane, hereditary sergeants of Carrick and kinsmen of the Bargany & Ardstinchar house, who used its walled-up cave as the local prison.

Until the Second World War, this stretch of land incorporated an 18-hole links course on both sides of the road.

The course was originally designed by William Fernie, the same Troon man who would later design the Turnberry course for the Marquess of Ailsa, and the Ballantrae Golf Club was formally instituted in 1877.

The names of only the 'best' holes of the course are known from The Golfing Annual of 1894:

- **Knockdolian** – *"A plateau 15 feet high, forty yards long and fifteen yards in diameter."* Named after a nearby hill known also as the 'False Craig' because it's so similar to Ailsa Craig.
- **Majuba Hill** – *"circled by precipitous sides."* Presumably named after the 1881 Battle of Majuba Hill, the main and decisive battle of the Boer War at which the British suffered a humiliating defeat. One or more of the local gentry may have been involved and lived on to rename a golf hole in its memory.
- **Half Way** – *"defended by two ravines, with a good lie between"*
- **The Saucer**
- **Purgatory** – *"out of which there is no redemption"*
- **Neck or Nothing / Hally's Circus** – *"intersected by the windings of the Red Burn which a player may do in 3, a novice 30."* The mention of the circus hole in the 1894 Golfing Annual precludes it from being named after anything in a Batman comic.

The same annual describes the course: *"The links are of the most varied and sporting description, mainly composed of the famed Ayrshire turf, comparatively free from 'traps', but abounding in hazards – sand bunkers, burns, ravines, ditches, and dykes guarding the holes. The approaches are well attended to, and an accurate game may be depended upon."*

Two famous authors left their mark on the village. Robert Louis Stevenson visited in the winter of 1876 and brought the name to worldwide attention by giving a novel the title *'The Master of Ballantrae'*. His friend Andrew Lang wrote about golf in his own famous novel *'A Monk of Fife'* set in the 15th century, which told the story of Joan of Arc from the point of view of the Book of Pluscarden's author, and it featured our Captain Hugh Kennedy.

We can suppose that Andrew Lang visited the village more than once. The Ballantrae Golf Club had *"the Hunter Monthly Medal, the Challenge Medal, the joint gift of Lord Archibald Campbell and Andrew Lang"* by 1888. He also mentioned the golf links when he wrote the poem *'Ballant o' Ballantrae'* and dedicated it to his friend Robert Louis Stevenson:

"Written in wet weather, this conveyed to the Master of Ballantrae a wrong idea of a very beautiful and charming place, **with links**..."

Andrew Lang, *'Ban and Arriere Ban'* – London 1894

But there's a much earlier mention of a links course in Ballantrae. In 1620, Thomas Kennedy of Bargany & Ardstinchar got into trouble for playing on it with a Kennedy relative who'd been proclaimed a rebel. The Register of the Privy Council of Scotland notes that Thomas *"keipit company, conferrence, and societie with the said rebell* **in the toun of Ballintra, playit with him on the linkis callit the grene of Ardstinchell..."**

Ardstinchar therefore had its very own links course 166 years after Hugh died, and it can only have been in the same place as the more recent course. Many of these Kennedys must have been early golfers, because there was also a cantankerous exchange of threatening letters after a previous Laird of Bargany (who died 1597) had his nose broken by a golf-ball whacked recklessly by the Laird of Culzean on the hills of Ayr – *"it was trewthe that his neise wes laich be ane straik of ane goiff-ball, on the hills of Air, in reklessnes"*.

Scotland's First GOLFER?
- Hugh Kennedy of Ardstinchar -

We don't know how long the links course called the Green of Ardstinchar had been in play by 1620, but it's interesting to note that those two descendants of Hugh's brother of Bargany & Ardstinchar are mentioned as early golfers...

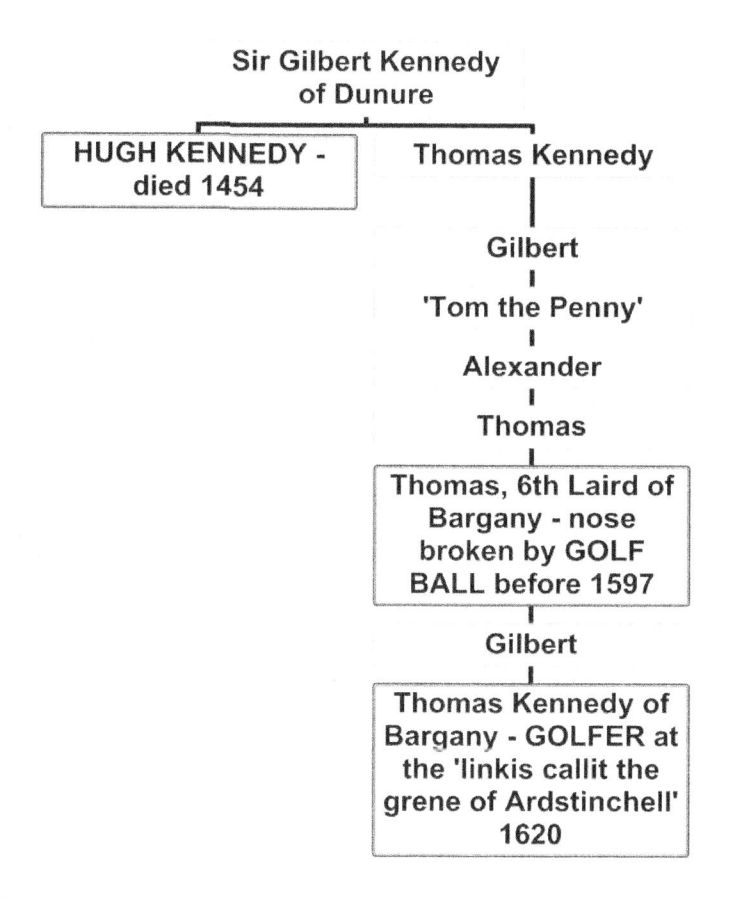

```
                Sir Gilbert Kennedy
                    of Dunure
        ┌───────────────┴───────────────┐
  HUGH KENNEDY -              Thomas Kennedy
     died 1454                       │
                                  Gilbert
                                     │
                              'Tom the Penny'
                                     │
                                 Alexander
                                     │
                                  Thomas
                                     │
                        ┌────────────────────────┐
                        │  Thomas, 6th Laird of  │
                        │   Bargany - nose       │
                        │   broken by GOLF       │
                        │   BALL before 1597     │
                        └────────────────────────┘
                                     │
                                  Gilbert
                                     │
                        ┌────────────────────────┐
                        │  Thomas Kennedy of     │
                        │  Bargany - GOLFER at   │
                        │  the 'linkis callit the│
                        │  grene of Ardstinchell'│
                        │          1620          │
                        └────────────────────────┘
```

...and that Hugh Kennedy himself was particularly well-placed in the prime links land of beachfront St Andrews when he returned to Scotland:

15th century
Timeline of Scottish Golf

| FOOTBALL BANNED | Hugh Kennedy in ST ANDREWS 1437 to 1454 | GOLF BANNED |

1421 1424   1430   1440   1450   1457

Battle of Baugé
"playing at ball"

Hugh's provostship of the Chapel Royal at Kirkheugh was for life, and it was just round the corner from the future site of the Royal and Ancient Course in the days before coastal erosion robbed even more land from the game.

He died in 1454 as Archdeacon of St Andrews, having just been called *'our beloved'* by King James II in a document, so he was in royal favour right to the end and mixing with the elite. Three years later that same king banned golf.

The game must have spread far and wide for it to be worth banning. Hugh was a wealthy man who moved in exalted circles. It's likely mere coincidence that our warrior churchman was in the right places at the right times – owning Ardstinchar where an early links course would come into official existence, and commuting between there for his castle building and St Andrews and France for his work.

But if you wanted to know how golf got started in 15th century Scotland, I'm sure the very man who could tell you would be Hugh Kennedy.

Scotland's First GOLFER?
- Hugh Kennedy of Ardstinchar -

In one of life's synchronicities – or a smile from beyond the grave – there are yet more parts to the story of golf tied to Hugh's village of Ballantrae. One began in 1977, the year Turnberry hosted the British Open and the epic battle of the 'Duel in the Sun' was fought between Jack Nicklaus and Tom Watson.

The names of Ballantrae and St Andrews were to be joined together again, this time in America.

Two golf-mad brothers from the USA were guests in my family home just a few yards along from Ardstinchar Castle, and drove to Turnberry each day. Chuck and Don Weber loved our wee Scottish village. Chuck being a real-estate developer, he was home less than a year before planning to use the name of Ballantrae for his condominium build at Delray Beach in Florida beside St Andrews golf club.

Letters and phone calls flew between the Webers and the Brittains. The developers wanted a tangible part of the Scottish Ballantrae to be built into their condo, so could we please freight over some stones from the beach? Indeed we did – 23 kilos of them. Some were to go into the foundations, and Chuck had ideas for others to go on a cairn or be encased in clear bricks within each home.

A letter from Chuck (Charles G Weber) in 1979 on St Andrews Corporation notepaper said *"The idea of the beach stones has captured the imagination of quite a few people we've spoken to"*.

A brochure for the condominium said:

"The six gentlemen of Scottish ancestry, who are the developers of St Andrews Club, are proud to present Ballantrae, their most splendid achievement...

...Ballantrae, as translated from the ancient Celtic tongue, means 'Village on the Shore'. The original village of Ballantrae on the Southwest coast of Scotland and the Firth of Clyde, has been there for over five hundred years; rich in heritage and steeped in tradition..."

My family lost touch with the Webers long ago, but an online search today shows the Ballantrae Condo complex built 1980 is still standing at North Ocean Boulevard.

Chuck only asked for the village's history after he'd gone home, and even then would never have learned of the 1620 **'linkis callit the grene of Ardstinchell'**. With the very reason for the Webers' visit being championship golf at Turnberry, it's such a shame he knew nothing of the Battle of Baugé and Ballantrae's own 15th century real-estate developer Hugh Kennedy being connected in print to the beginnings of Scottish golf.

The name of Ballantrae is popular around the world. Nearly all of the instances originate from our wee Ayrshire village, sometimes from Robert Louis Stevenson's use of it for his novel after his visit. It's particularly grand to see the name being used for several golf courses in the USA and Canada. A brief peek now shows:

- **Ballantrae Golf Club** – Pelham, Alabama
- **Ballantrae, a golf and yachting community** – Port Saint Lucie, Florida
- **Ballantrae Park & Residential Golf Community** – Dublin, Ohio
- **Ballantrae Golf Club** – Stouffville, Ontario
- **Maples of Ballantrae Golf Club** – Stouffville, Ontario

If Hugh Kennedy was indeed involved in any way with the development of Scottish golf in St Andrews and the pioneering beginnings of the Ardstinchar links course, I think he'd be well pleased to know of this Ballantrae diaspora far beyond the horizon in miles and years. He'd certainly feel right at home on the Pelham course where there's a castellated turret beside the water!

ABOUT THE AUTHOR

Jean Brittain, BA, FSA Scot, grew up in Ballantrae next to the ruins of Hugh Kennedy's castle of Ardstinchar. Previously a college lecturer and bookshop manager, she specialises in Scotland's history and folklore and is the author of over fifty magazine and newspaper articles.

For illustrated talks to groups, clubs and historical societies please contact jeanbrittain@gmail.com

NOTES & SELECT BIBLIOGRAPHY

Scottish Golf History

R Browning, *A History of Golf: The Royal and Ancient Game* – London 1955

O M Geddes, *A Swing Through Time: Golf in Scotland 1457-1744* – Edinburgh 2007

'Origins of Golf' – British Golf Museum at St Andrews –
www.britishgolfmuseum.co.uk/the-collections/origins-of-golf/

For the original Ballantrae Golf Club instituted 1877, see the informative website Golf's Missing Links -
www.golfsmissinglinks.co.uk/index.php/scotland-63/south/ayrshire/102-ballantrae-golf-club-ayrshire

Fascinating in-depth articles and commentary by Neil Laird –
www.scotttishgolfhistory.org

'The linkis callit the Grene of Ardstinchel':
The Register of the Privy Council of Scotland, Vol 12 – Edinburgh 1895

Kennedy of Bargany's nose broken by a golf ball:
R Pitcairn   *'Historical and Genealogical Account of the Principal Families of the Name of Kennedy, from an Original Manuscript'* – Edinburgh 1830.

Kennedy History

'Thom the Penny' is in National Records of Scotland GD25/1/617. All credit for the discovery of this man's true identity goes to James Brown who happened across Tom while researching the Kennedy history of his own Baltersan Castle.

R Pitcairn – *'Historical and Genealogical Account of the Principal Families of the Name of Kennedy, from an Original Manuscript'* – Edinburgh 1830

Original manuscript: *The Historie of the Kennedyis*, ADV MS 33.3.28 at the National Library of Scotland

J Brittain & J Brown, *'And uther placis'* – *Two French ambassadorial missions in Ayrshire* – Scottish Local History Journal, Issue 94, 2016

J Balfour Paul, *Scots Peerage, Volume 2* – 1905

Military, Church and General History

B Ditcham, *The Employment of Foreign Mercenary Troops in the French Royal Armies 1415-1470* – PhD Dissertation, University of Edinburgh, 1978

F Skene (Editor), *The Book of Pluscarden* – Edinburgh 1880

F D Logan, *Runaway Religious in Medieval England, c1240-1540* – Cambridge 2002

W Forbes-Leith, *The Scots Men-At-Arms and Life-Guards in France* – Edinburgh 1882

Francisque-Michel, *Les Ecossais en France, Les Français en Ecosse* – London 1862

The Chronicles of Enguerrand de Monstrelet: Vol 1 – London 1853

J-A Le Paire, *Annales du Pays de Lagny* – Lagny-sur-Marne 1880

Scotland's First GOLFER?
- Hugh Kennedy of Ardstinchar -

L Barbé, *Margaret of Scotland & The Dauphin Louis* – London 1917

C Hare, *The Life of Louis XI* – London 1907

K Ralls, *The Templars and the Grail* – USA 2003

Father R A Hay, *Genealogie of the Sainteclaires of Rosslyn* (Edited by R L D Cooper) – Edinburgh 2002

D E R Watt (Editor), *Scotichronicon by Walter Bower in Latin and English: Vol 8* – Aberdeen 1987

Oxbrow & Robertson, *Rosslyn and the Grail* – Edinburgh 2006

A Kerr, *'The Collegiate Church or Chapel of Rosslyn, its Builders, Architect, and Construction'* in Proceedings of the Society of Antiquaries of Scotland, Vol 12 – Edinburgh 1877

Kennedy Mausoleum (Bargany Aisle) mason may have been David Scougal:
http://churchmonumentssociety.org/MonumentoftheMonthArchive/2011-02.html

C Wright, *The Maze and the Warrior: Symbols in Architecture, Theology and Music* – London 2001

ACKNOWLEDGEMENTS

Conjectural reconstruction of Ardstinchar Castle – from original artwork by **Andrew Spratt**

Hugh Kennedy's heraldic shield showing single fleur-de-lys quartered with Kennedy – from original graphic by **Ben Kennedy**

Theseus and the Minotaur, King Charles VII, King James I – Wikimedia Commons License

Photo of turret on Ballantrae Golf Course, Pelham, USA – courtesy of **James Helton**

Photo of golfers on Ballantrae Links Golf Course, Scotland – courtesy of **Keith & Christine Brown**

Photo of Ballantrae Condominium in Florida – sent 1979 to Mr & Mrs W Brittain from Charles Weber, Vice President, St Andrews Corporation, Delray Beach, Florida USA

My thanks to author **Fiona McLaren** for reading draft and making helpful suggestions.

Jean Brittain's full biography

HUGH KENNEDY OF ARDSTINCHAR
Joan of Arc's Scottish Captain

is available on Amazon Kindle and iTunes

ISBN: 978-0-9570363-4-5

Published by Brodie Books 2012

Scotland's First GOLFER?
- Hugh Kennedy of Ardstinchar -

Please feel welcome to contact the author at
jeanbrittain@gmail.com

www.facebook.com/HughKennedyOfArdstinchar

Printed in Great Britain
by Amazon